positively

hope you enjoy!

PAW ELEMENTARY:
ROXY'S ADVENTURE TO THE SCHOOL DENTIST

written by Katie Melko

illustrated by Roksana Oslizlo

12 Paws Publishing LLC

ISBN - 978-1-5323-9282-5

Illustrated by Roksana Oslizlo

Printed in China

First Edition

To my Roxy girl

Roxy was two months into kindergarten at Paw Elementary School. She loved school and all the new friends she'd made so far.

One day, her school announced the dentist would be coming to visit to check everyone's teeth and make sure they're healthy.

Mrs. Jasmine, Roxy's teacher, instructed the students to have their parents fill out a permission slip and return it the next day. As her classmates were talking, Roxy realized this would be her first visit to the dentist – and she was getting scared.

That night, Roxy went home and showed mama and papa the form. After reading it, they agreed this would be good for Roxy.

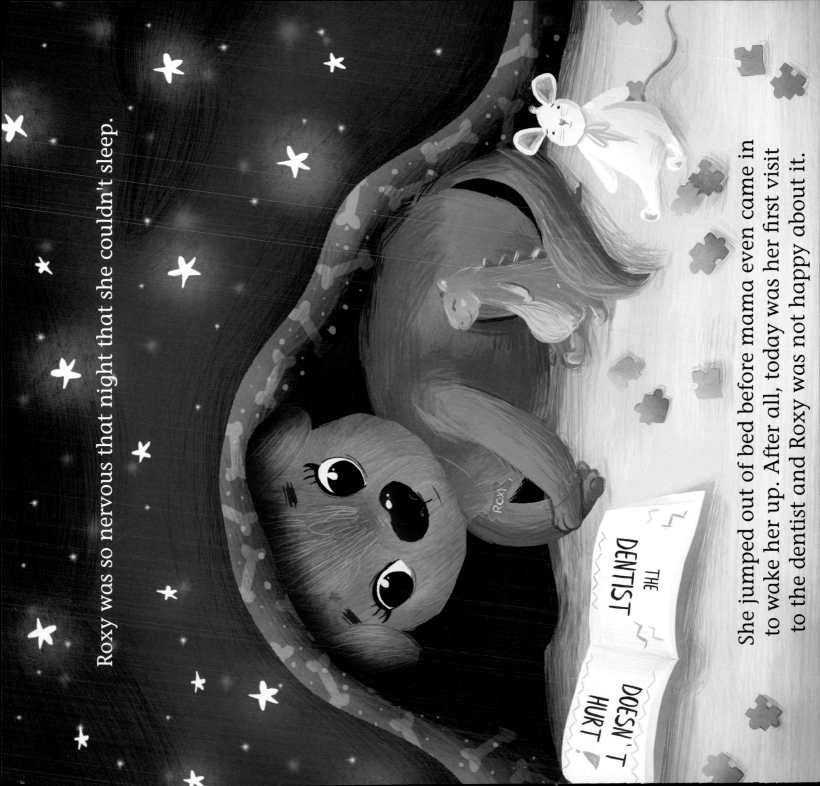

Roxy was so nervous that night that she couldn't sleep.

She jumped out of bed before mama even came in to wake her up. After all, today was her first visit to the dentist and Roxy was not happy about it.

THE DENTIST DOESN'T HURT

You see, Roxy's brother, Mason, was telling her scary stories about the dentist. He'd teased her all night, telling her they were going to pull out all her teeth and she wouldn't be able to eat!

Mama tried to tell her that Mason was only joking and she would be OK, but Roxy was worried. She grabbed her backpack and gave mama a hug and a kiss. Mama then waved goodbye and told her to have a great day.

As Roxy walked to school with her friend, Noel, that morning, she asked her if she'd ever been to the dentist. "Yeah," said Noel. "My mom took me because my tooth hurt and the dentist pulled it out!"

Oh no! This was not what Roxy wanted to hear. She shook her head the whole way to school thinking about how the dentist might start pulling her teeth.

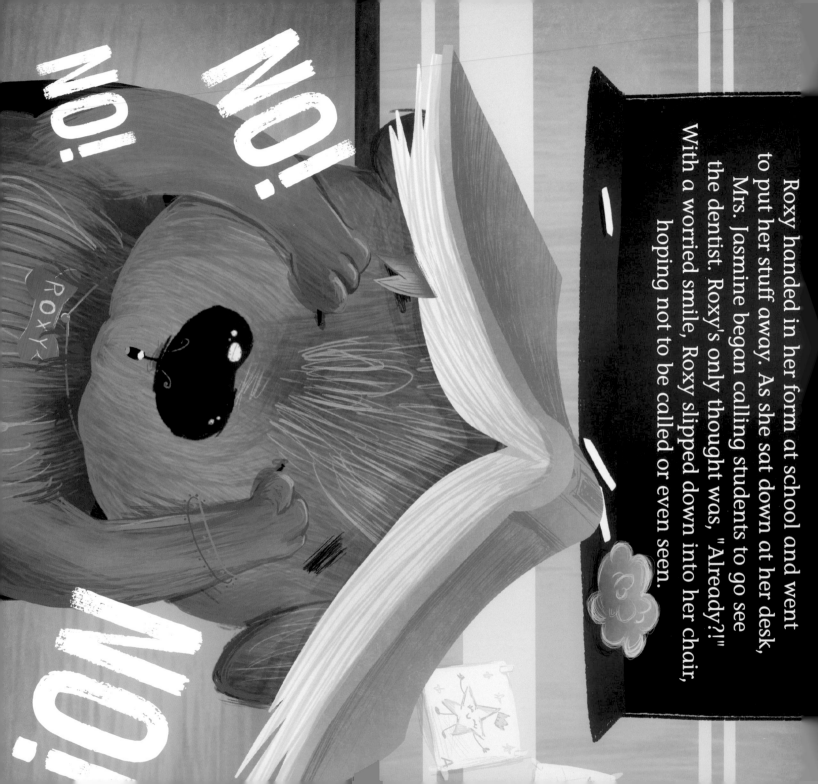

Roxy handed in her form at school and went to put her stuff away. As she sat down at her desk, Mrs. Jasmine began calling students to go see the dentist. Roxy's only thought was, "Already?!" With a worried smile, Roxy slipped down into her chair, hoping not to be called or even seen.

As her classmate, Astoria, looked at her and asked,
"Is everything OK?", she heard Mrs. Jasmine say,
"Roxy, please go to room B57 to see the dentist."
"No, no, no," Roxy thought. "It's too soon."
But her teacher patted Roxy on the back
and, with a smile on her face said, "Have fun!"

"Fun?" Roxy questioned as she walked down the hall. "That's not possible." Thankfully, her friend, Luna, was going with her, too. Together, they walked slowly to the dentist, hoping to take as long as possible to reach the room.

As Roxy and Luna walked into the room, they could see two dental chairs and heard loud noises coming from the machines. It looked really scary, but no one was upset or even crying.

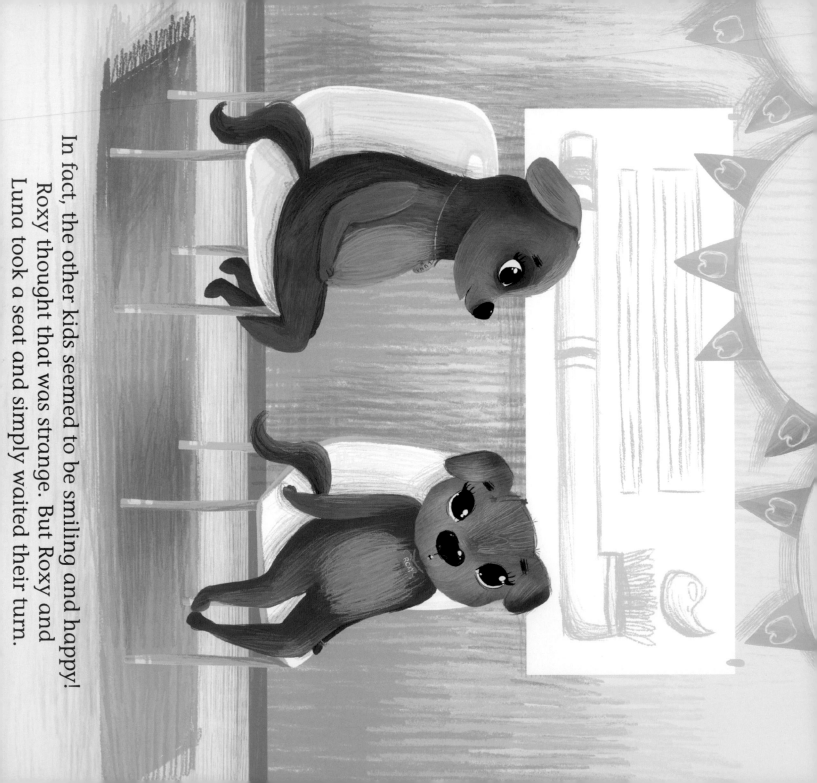

In fact, the other kids seemed to be smiling and happy! Roxy thought that was strange. But Roxy and Luna took a seat and simply waited their turn.

She thought about everything she could see in the room, when a woman greeted her and asked for her name. "Roxy Mesko," she said. But the woman asked again, "I couldn't hear you, what was that dear?" Roxy repeated herself and the woman asked, "Are you nervous, sweetie?" And Roxy shook her head yes.

"Well, my name is Tide and I'm a dental hygienist," said the nice woman. "Please, don't be nervous. This will be easy and pain free! Come with me." Roxy looked up at her with a sense of relief and followed her to the chair. But Roxy didn't know what to do as she stared and wondered what the tools were for.

Tide told her to sit in what looked like a long beach chair. As Roxy looked around, Tide said, "Don't worry, I'll tell you what everything is!" Roxy hadn't lost any teeth yet and wondered what Tide was going to do. Was she going to pull them out?

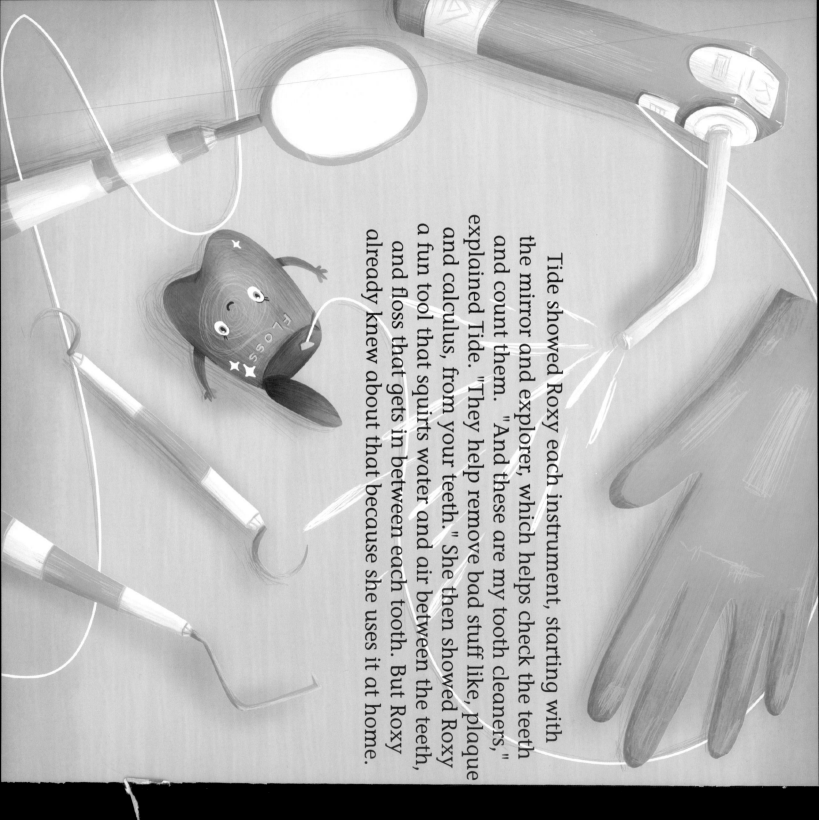

Tide showed Roxy each instrument, starting with the mirror and explorer, which helps check the teeth and count them. "And these are my tooth cleaners," explained Tide. "They help remove bad stuff like, plaque and calculus, from your teeth." She then showed Roxy a fun tool that squirts water and air between the teeth, and floss that gets in between each tooth. But Roxy already knew about that because she uses it at home.

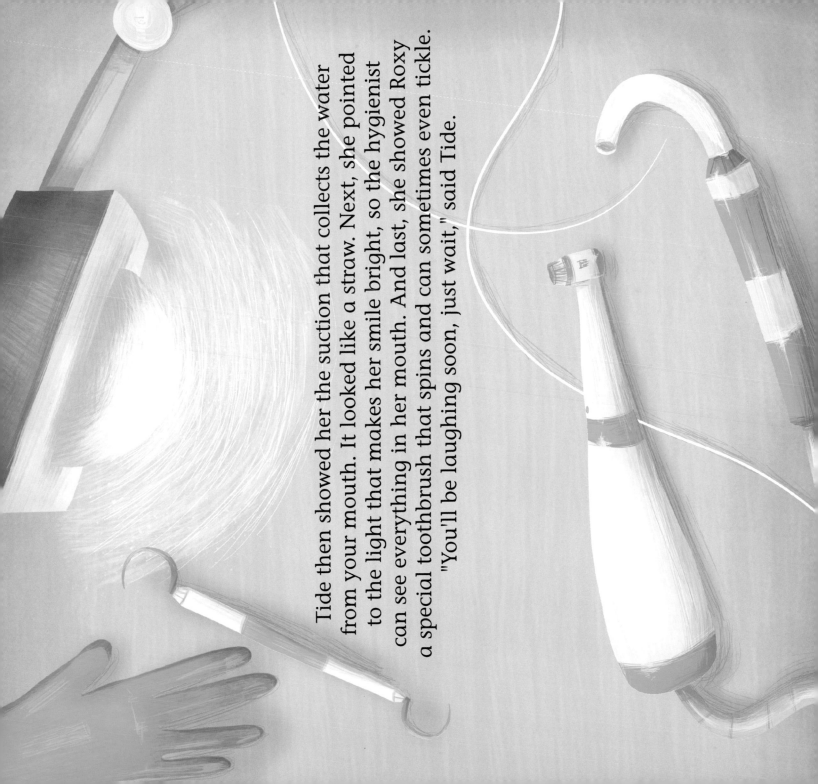

Tide then showed her the suction that collects the water from your mouth. It looked like a straw. Next, she pointed to the light that makes her smile bright, so the hygienist can see everything in her mouth. And last, she showed Roxy a special toothbrush that spins and can sometimes even tickle. "You'll be laughing soon, just wait," said Tide.

And Tide was right. The cleaning was actually easy and fun. Roxy learned that she has 20 baby teeth and two of her six-year adult molars had grown in, but those needed sealants. "Need what?" Roxy asked nervously. "Sealants," Tide said. "They help protect the teeth from cavities, which damage your teeth and make them weak!"

After the cleaning, Tide took two pictures of Roxy's teeth. She explained that these pictures are called X-rays and they help the dentist see in between the teeth. You see, cavities hide between the teeth and the hygienist can't see in those tiny spaces when looking in the mouth. But the X-rays show everything. Roxy thought this was really cool and she even got to see her own X-rays!

After taking the pictures, Tide taught Roxy how and when to brush, and the importance of flossing.

Tide told her to brush every morning and night, for 2 minutes each time. Roxy knew mama would help her with that!

Next, Tide told Roxy that the dentist, Dr. Harley, was going to look at her teeth, too. Tide promised her it wouldn't hurt at all. Since Roxy trusted her, she tried not to be scared and stayed calm. Dr. Harley came into the room, said hi and quickly made her laugh, as she looked at Roxy's teeth. "This isn't so bad," Roxy thought.

Dr. Harley told Roxy she was cavity-free and had her first wiggly tooth. Roxy was so excited. She didn't even know she'd be losing a tooth soon! Tide gave Roxy a cool new toothbrush and a sticker before she left to go back to class. "Wow," thought Roxy. She had learned a lot today about her teeth and it was so easy.

As she walked back to class, Roxy thought about how she'd worried all night and day about something that was actually fun! And when Roxy ran into her friend, Brandi, on the way back to class, she told her not to be scared, because she knew she'd be smiling on her way back, too!

Roxy was so excited to get home and share the great news with mama and tell Mason about everything she'd learned today. "He'll be so impressed," Roxy thought.

Looking back, Roxy realized that going to the dentist wasn't scary at all. Turns out, it was fun and hygienists keep our teeth clean and healthy! Tide told Roxy she should see the dentist twice a year. And because Roxy knows hygienists and dentists are here to help keep your smile bright, she'll be looking forward to her next adventure to see the dentist.